AF424684

Before you shed my blood
Poetry book
Written by the poet and novelist
khalil altahhan

Before you shed my blood
Poetry book
Written by the poet and novelist
Khalil altahhan
"Syrian author"

Also by khalil altahhan:

Before you shed my blood

Diary of a Damascene wound

Te Prophecy of the Eternal Winter.

Tears of angels

<u>introduction</u>

Creativity is the legitimate child of sadness
Most of the poems that entered history from its widest
chapters studied at the University of Sorrows
"the poem" When she was young, she was a student at the
School of Sadness
Then she graduated with merit
She received a master's degree and an honorary doctorate in
the Department of depression and tears
This is the true birth of the wonderful poem
But the poem in this book is a little different
She has been singing about love in her past
And on this rotten earthly apple
There is no creature outcast, miserable, with torn clothes,
An orphan, a refugee, a homeless, hungry, and thrown on the
sidewalks ,, More than love
The poem was studied in the school of sadness
But her school was destroyed
She is a survivor of the war
and came out from the rubble
She went far beyond the stage of grief and declared holy war
Oh, rich and emotional reader
This book is very rough
It may bleed on your hands

This book is packed with out-of-the-box ideas
And very aggressive in the face of herd instinct
This book contains poems wanted dead or alive
Every poem in this book is pursued
by Hulagu's guards
O reader, who is resting on the bed of illusion
My poems may dance for you and seduce you
But be careful
Every poem in this book is an angry ghost of a dead woman
who has returned to take revenge on those who killed her
Every poem in this book is a Female suicide bomber
Wearing an explosive belt
And you, O sleeper, over the pieces of his conscience
My poems will not come to you to knock on your door to tell
you
Please wake up
But it will destroy your home
....
It should be noted

<u>They threatened me</u>
They trampled on me
and gouged out my eyes
When I said yes, I was killed
When I said no, they raped me
They called me a terrorist
Others called me a heretic
They recorded my statements
while I was silent
Then they said kill him
After they called me a traitor
The people are oppressed and hungry
And they hate each other
And they hate me
My crime was:
love
And they don't understand me
***

A killer wants
To free us from the butcher

A fraudster enters the mosque
And to every temple
A trifle who insults, curses,
and laughs at the minds of a nation of billions
And an army enters the cities as a conqueror
To go out on a donkey
Leaving behind what was a city
And there was destruction
A ridiculous person describes half the people as
heretic
While playing gambling!!
A loser rides on people's backs
He plays with the feelings of the revolutionaries
A revolution like fast food!!
Antara wants to free us from Shahryar
A thief defending our rights
In the face of the broker
An unknown person who was one of the worst
villains before the revolution
They took him out of prison in a general amnesty
Today you see him fighting with the free people

And you want victory from God!!?
What an irony of fate!!
***

A stripper who defected from the army!
She was almost a prophet in the eyes of the
revolutionaries
They honored her
and wrote her name
On the first pages
They chanted her name in slogans
They beat the drums for her
She was a prophet for the regime
Today she has become a crazy person to them
Omar bin Al-Khattab did not join the revolution
In the eyes of the revolutionaries
he became an ogre
God is confused about
who to stand with
In both cases he will be killed
And Abu Lahab guides whomever He wishes
He misleads whomever He wills!

The presence of Satan in Heaven has become reasonable

***

People eat waste
If their condition improves, they eat beans
And the rich you see in bars
In solidarity with those who were martyred
The insignificant poet writes the most insignificant phrases
It becomes acceptable to his supporters
And a fraud that worships pagan idols
He becomes a sheikh
He explains the basics of religion to people
Abu Jahl announces his conversion to Islam
And he manipulates the verses
He shouts "Allahu Akbar" masculinely
Suddenly, a person who was an unknown junk seller comes out before the revolution
He claims to be educated
On the back of those who were killed in the revolution...

He thinks he is Shakespeare and a womanizer of
manhood
He messes everything up
Those who were once dead
They officially entered the tomb today
Whoever did not die with the right sword was
struck with the left hand
And whoever is not eaten by the wolf
He was eaten by the lion
***

Oh my poor country
You dead people
O you who were immersed in humiliation and
submission yesterday
Victory comes from God
He gives it to the pure
He guides them to the right path
He prevents victory from the immoral and
scoundrel insulters
You will not be victorious as long as there is all this
corruption in your hearts

You will not be victorious unless you purify yourselves of grudges

~~~~~
~~~~~

"Thanks be to God, Lord of all worlds"

We bleed by saying "There is no power nor
strength except with God"
with the shoes on our heads we say "Amen"
In the name of God, we eat garbage
Is there more clay than this clay?
Rich people drink whiskey and eat caviar
We drink slime and eat flip flops
Scoundrels build palaces and enjoy money
We live in graves and ruins
Bribed people enjoy Gordon Bleu
As for us, if we see the loaf, we think it is a
crescent moon
Thank God it is a blessing and everything is fine
The country is in good condition
The cameras film a smiling citizen and another
walking around the Al-Hal Market
Everything is perfect with us
Everything is going well
The competent authorities take care of everything
And if they wanted to move mountains

The army married the people halally
And they lived happily and contentedly
They had many children
Terrorism was crushed and we died
... Why? this is the question!
Our skin become peeled and cracked
From stabs and knives
We becames skinny from hunger
And God loves those who are patient!
impalements are Messing with our asses
A thousand motherfuckers made it for us
We can barely get the impalement out of our asses
And if we see ourselves as prisoners
We can hardly get out of prison
Except we are surprised by a group of killers
We would hardly finish these things without being
bombed
We become homeless on the streets
And when we survive all these disasters
The impalement himself is waiting for us, smiling
And we sit on it

We cannot spit, cry, or curse the heaven
Otherwise, they will call us unbelievers
Our homes were destroyed, our dreams were torn
apart
And all my poor neighbors
Is this really our beautiful neighborhood?
Or is it Hiroshima?
Does the commander know about this?
The Great Conqueror "Commander of the Faithful"
Does the Almighty One know that?
Does the One and Only One, the most just of all,
know this?
A person comes to us with a cigar in his mouth
We hear what he says while we are on the
impalement in silence
He wears a turban and takes out the rosary from his
pocket
The sign of prayer appears on his forehead
Suddenly he becomes one of the religious
He looks at us with sadness and a light shines from
his face

And in his eyes is the humility of the humble
He stands over us while we are thrown on the
ground in front of him like bags of flour
He says: Brother, why are you upset?
Be patient and have peace and trust in God, the
Most Merciful
The impalement is a blessing. Sit on it
And Be thankful. my brother in religion
I tell him: I want you to deliver a message on
behalf of me
and all the poor people on the sidewalks
On behalf of millions...
He says what is the message and to whom: so I say
We are a people who only prostrate to God
He says: Is this the matter?
He shakes his head, smiling like a motherfucker
I say to him: We are a people who are patient for
God
Not for the general or the Commander of the
Faithful
So tell him on my behalf

and on behalf of all these refugees
Tell him to have mercy on people so that God will
have mercy on him
We are so unbearably weak and poor
We are very tired
This poverty, this oppression, and this humiliation
are very, very degrading
He shakes his head again and throws away his cigar
And I fall to the ground, me and my sad
impalement

~~~~~
~~~~~

The birth of rain

Don't ask me how many times I've been killed
I found myself in the ambulance
Why ? I didn't know
What I remember
I was sitting in my house
Suddenly I was bombed
I had little dreams
I lost all of them
***

I am a poor citizen of Damascus
I live as much as I can
I believe everything they say
And I hear everything that is rumored
My thought is simple...and my reward is little
And my family is hungry
I walk from wall to wall
I wear a mask of my isolation
I didn't care.. I didn't understand
Whether they say revolution or they say deception
I believe in bread

And from the news I get a headache
Like any simple person
I dream of a warm homeland...and a love that
cannot be sold
Hours ago, it was my mother
She weaves wool and listens to the radio
My brothers were playing
And now everything is lost
***

Before the disaster happens
I was likeable in my neighborhood
I was simple human being.
It was the best thing in my life
My work..and my pillow
I didn't go to cafes
I was always passing by restaurants
After work as usual
I dreamed of being there one day
with that beautiful girl I loved
she was my neighbor
***

The restaurant and café are now demolished
The people of my neighborhood were displaced
The place became deserted
They kidnapped and killed my beloved
So what should I say, my friends?
How do I explain my condition to you!!
***

on behalf of this poor person
I will write...
And I will give the banner of revolution to the
poem
on behalf of every hungry person
I will declare disobedience
ladies and gentlemen
***

on behalf of all the homeless without homes
In the name of all the lost
Between oppression and hunger
And farces
And on behalf of those who have never known
what the sun looks like

who lived and died in vain
In the name of those who missed the train
They tasted nothing but dust
Under bombing, killing and earthquakes
on behalf of the unjustly imprisoned
who terrifies the jailer
Despite the yoke and chains
on behalf of every oppressed person
The poem will wear the dress of a fighter
My country will not die
We will plant thousands of ears of corn on its land
***

Dear people
Prepare the wood stove
The rain is sure to fall
People, do not despair
The night will end

~~~~~
~~~~~

<u>What use are words anymore?</u>

They left and betrayed
they were ruined and died
And it's over
The homeland is dying on the bed of oppression
And his foolish sons prepare the mourning garment
Everything is ready...the coffin and the gravedigger
And a knife to stab him if he doesn't die
Their mother, Syria, laments her bad luck
They forced her to wear black
They shortened her waiting period..
They want to marry her quickly to the son of a liver
eater
What use are words anymore?
Poems are no longer useful
At the funeral, all languages die
The sons sold the house, the roof and the walls
They inherited the country during his lifetime
They threw their mother into the well
And they dressed the wolf as a sheikh
They glued a beard to him

To read some verses of the Qur'an
On a moonless night
The wolf sneaked in and raped with all the
daughters
Then he went out to the wedding hall, smiling
And behold, he himself was the groom, the son of
the liver-eater
Those present congratulated him and rejoiced over
him
They prayed for him to be happy and prosperous
Syria shouts: This wedding is not my wedding
This shame is not my shame
..Stay away from me, you bastards
But..what use are words anymore?
And the forbidden fills us from head to toe
Mud, fall, villainy, and corruption
We oppressed our father, the homeland... we hated
him... we stroked him
And we fored our mother "syria"
to marry the wolf
because of grudges

What use are words anymore?
The poem choked and the ink dried up
The papers became black
This era is a bad drummer
and people dressed as strippers
This era is gay...and it sings!
and People loved the ugliest sounds
I came back from my slow death
After the hands of fate buried me alive
I returned from...and to a world that taught me
To walk alone in silence
To search for my life..
because I lost history, love, and homeland
The roads chew me and the sun burns me
Summer is stupid and the trees are inanimate
Damascus is like a child singing under the bridge
They throw some liras in front of her
Between Qasioun and Ghouta there is a story that
hurt me
They separated after a love that lasted millions of
years

They threw Aleppo into the pit
They threw the wolf with her
After all the scoundrels raped her
Now on the other sidewalk in the trail
Exhausted from fatigue
And Homs, with her torn dress, is reaping
A tax on her beauty like all beauties
She sells roses with a dream and a wish in her eyes
That the days of mourning end
Raqqa is in the slave market, pulled by a sheikh
pimp
The world is perverted
but the female "Syria" hated that life
The world is an ugly old man who has lost his
manhood
Without purpose, he strips beautiful women
O God of heaven, help me
To reap this harvest with my country
I returned from my death
to the Syria that left me
With a love that has passed away

Carrying on my back sorrows that broke me
And a heavy burden of memories
I came back and people were looking at me
as if I am coming from the time of prophecies
I crossed places and I thought
That I will plant the seeds of life in my heart
But the places tired me, strangled me, and
disfigured me
All of them, like my heart, have become ashes

~~~~~
~~~~~

<u>Autobiography of an unhappy poet</u>
<u>"1"</u>

I always sat alone
In the ways of sorrows
I was smoking my cigarette
While I was waiting for the train of time
I was hanging out alone
In cafes with unknown address
I was drinking my coffee
I was drinking my disappointment
From that cup
I used to spend my isolation in the cafes of my city
Between the shisha and the smoke haze
I was wasting my time
In places that have no place
Sometimes at the watermelon seller
And sometimes at the bakery
Sometimes because of debt
I was avoiding passing by the grocery store
I was leaving the greengrocer
Abu Abdo

To go to the barber, Abu Hassan
I was talking to my neighbor Abu Tahseen
About the price of tomatoes and the high prices
And sometimes he says to me
What will you get from bullshit of writing poems,
you idiot?
Leave poetry and open a shop
Imagine!!
The poet is in my country to live
He must work as a janitor
And the musician to buy a loaf of bread
He works as a drummer during Ramadan suhoor
My beautiful neighbor
Her name was Susan
She was watching me from the window every time
she saw me
Her brother hits her
He killed her in an honor killing
May God's curse be upon this man
Then he went out in a demonstration for freedom!
He disappeared and no one knows where he is yet

And my mean neighbor
I knew her for a long time
She sometimes sold flowers
And bread in front of the bakery
Her father is a fraud, her mother is a beggar
And her boyfriend is in the army
My second neighbor is an informer
He worked as a smuggled smoke seller
Then he joined the revolutionaries and founded a
battalion
Some thugs joined him
Then he returned to the army
and lived happily and stole tons
Don't worry about the story...
Everything is jumbled and random
Our neighborhood is simple and does not interfere
in politics
And God is the Helper
..My second neighbor
Her name was Razan
She dreamed of becoming a singer and traveling to

Lebanon
She dreamed of marrying a Mercedes owner
Or even Nissan
I dated her once
The other time she didn't come
She found out that I was a poor man
I return from my appointment disappointed and
delirious
And I put my head on my pillow
Tomorrow I will start my journey again
I thank God for the blessing of forgetfulness
One day I met a girl named Rawan
Is that really her name?
not important
Her eyes are like pearls
And her lips are like coral
I loved her...she loved me
Her love surprised me
But after a while
She showed me the stars at noon
In the end she left me

And married an idiot!
then
I became as emotionless as a crocodile
I got used to sadness
It no longer affects me
No earthquakes or hurricanes
Not even a volcano
"And I became a poet
Audiences applaud me everywhere!
I woke up from my sleep
I took a cigarette from a smoke packet
I remembered my neighbor's advice
But it was too late
I left my house full of hope
To collect the price of the vegetable shop
And the story is over

~~~~~
~~~~~

<u>Autobiography of an unhappy poet</u>
<u>"2"</u>

O my reader, if I disbelieve one day, do not blame
me
Even if I scream at the top of my voice
If I curse a little, do not blame me
And on the face of this era I spat
Reader, forgive me
Because this is how my poem began
Read my poetry, but don't ask me about it
I don't remember what I wrote myself
I did my poems because I...
I wrote it when I got drunk
And here it is in your hands, but I...
I laughed a lot because of my crying
I have a girlfriend who had sex with me
And on the heights of her breasts I was crucified
I brutally raped her one day
Then I became a hermit when I woke up
She thanked me for my action and kissed me
And I forgot what I did

I have a girlfriend whom I loved, but she wronged
me
I don't remember that I ever wronged her
and i have a luck that always run away from me
To the ends of the world
I have an audience that reads my poetry and art
They are ten if you count
And I have a bitch who liked me
Her butt so big I was amazed
I remember the first time she tald to me
I read my poetry to her
But she yawned and silenced me
But she was very happy when I danced
I won't lie to you, she fooled me
But I was very happy with her
I'll tell you what I did next
There was a revolution in my city that surprised me
I don't remember that I ever demonstrated
What I remember is that I woke up and...
I found blood on my shirt
On Al Jazeera, they said I was a thug

On government channels, they said that I was a
terrorist
They filmed me burning the police station
they told: Half of the demonstrators i was killed
But I don't think so
I don't remember doing so
Just what I remember
I wrote poetry, drank vodka, and slept
I received a message on my phone
Throw away your pen and don't write! But I didn't
do it
An army battalion threatened me
And half the neighborhood, but I laughed
The seller of smuggled smoke complained about
me
He bargained with me and I told him to go to hell
My fat neighbor woman threatened me
Your name is required, so follow me
So I said to the officer at the checkpoint: Arrest me
I am a criminal and armed
But surprisingly, he didn't believe me

So to the Free Army I went
The gunman said to me: Stay away from me
So I heard him a poem from the last thing she
wrote
But when he heard it, he ran away from me
And I finally gave up
My reader, do not quote this from me
Don't tell anyone what you did
Forget this poem and do not blame me
I did not write and you did not read

~~~~~
~~~~~

<u>Who am I in a time of overthrow, falling and the fallen?</u>

I am a great witness to the era
I entered palaces of gold
I slept on a silk bed
I wandered through streets full of oppression, cold, and sleet
I was the king through my heart and my poetry
My poetry, which is bigger than any big one
And here I am now as always
I'm sitting on the sidewalk with a poor man
The whirlwinds passed by me
The vegetable seller and the prostitute passed by
A caller to Islam and a caller to Christianization
The one I loved and the one I hated have passed
..and many, many more
Someone passed by who was reckless with my sitting
The one who threatened to kill me just because I was sitting passed by
Those who incited me, those who oppressed me,

and those who threatened me passed by
More than one villain passed
Those who financed me and those who betrayed me
passed
I didn't care about them, they were all donkeys
When I expressed my opinion
They all came to kill me
As long as they are democratic and free
So why do they silence me? What is the
explanation?
I remained standing still
And if I walk, I know where I'm going
I am the poet on the sidewalk
Next to me is a beggar, and we sit on a mat
Who is greater than us but God?
Me and this poor man
Who is imposing on us what to do?
Disgraced is every hired usurer
You will not hear my voice in this despicable,
polluted time
And if you hear him, he will burn you all

And you will see from my poetry the burning fire
I wanted her before you were born, a revolution for
Jasmine
Roses and birds share it
I previously wanted it to be a revolution to create a
republic of love
A soft revolution of femininity and fragrance
Remember when I announced my revolution?
You all stood against me
And you said that I am a crazy, drunken magician
Do you remember when I started my revolution?
You stoned me and expelled me from my tribe
I saw a lot of injustice from you
Where were you?
You have been watching a drama
You were falling as martyrs for the sake of
Muhannad and Lamis
With unparalleled absurdity
Your former heroes, what happened to them?
Are they now worthless in your opinion?
Neither Murad Alam Dar or akid

nor anyone else will save you
They are stone idols, and you have a small mind
You're building a shrine to every silly person
And you sanctify the fraudster
And you make him a prince
You do not know your head from your feet
Yesterday's hero, in your opinion, today is
despicable
And the hero of the day, who knows?
In your opinion, he may become a villain tomorrow
As for me, you always hate me and are against me
Because I know you well
And expose you well
And always point out your faults
I don't claim my self to be flawless
But who claims freedom and suppresses my
opinion?
This is the dangerous thing
Even those I defended stood against me
They said I was just a bastard
Who do I mean? I will say all of you

You who raise the slogans of freedom and change
My revolution is white and it was before you
Who are you to impose on me where I should go?
I am with myself...and my poetry is a constitution
Who is worthy in this filthy time to guide me where
I should go?
Only God can command me
I am the people and I am the government
I am the poet and also this poor man
My revolution is clean, so be with me
Instead of killing and destroying
Preach the culture of love
If you really want to change
This is my revolution
To create a new generation that respects the rose,
the book of poetry, and femininity
And every butterfly flies
I reject your revolution
Which rejects this poem of mine
Then you claim freedom of expression
If you say we are the ones to be killed

Who knows who the killer is?
Everyone masters the art of forgery
It doesn't matter who gets killed
If blood flows, whatever it is, then change is
miserable
curse yourselves in your homes
You restrict your children and restrict your women
You who killed your sister or your wife with an
honor killing
then you commit adultery on the same bed
Don't be ashamed of yourself
And you are the one demanding change
O sheikh who gives fatwas for customary marriage
and recklessly interprets verses
and gives fatwas for breastfeeding an elderly men.
When Gaza was dying, you were distracted by
fatwas
on how to go to the bathroom and drink camel
urine.
Now you come to kill me
O breed of sheep and donkeys

Because I stand neutral between my brother and my
cousin
and listen to the voice of conscience
Do you give a fatwa to kill me if I scream:
Beware of Al-Basous
And if I shouted at Jassas
My voice became hoarse as I told him:
it is dangerous for you to kill your cousin
Is this freedom... how ironic!
In this time, someone who does not distinguish
between lamb and barley wants to teach me
freedom.
Glory be to Him who said
Are those who know and those who do not know
equal?
Glory be to Him, All-Seeing of people
If I am not with you, then I am against you
Screw this blatant and despicable principle
Kill yourself before you give a fatwa to kill me
If I did not follow your desire
Who appointed you as Lord?

To issue death sentences and accuse people of
disbelief?
I reject you, my dear sheikh
I reject all of your Islam
It is all forgery
Islam is greater than all the parasites that distort it,
such as cockroaches
Christ said:
Love your enemies and bless those who curse you
Consider this great speech
He said it and they all rejected him, preachers of
hatred
then he had no supporter left
And the Qur'an says, "Repel with goodnes."
And let them pardon and forgive
This is the word of God and not words of man
I reject you all
And for your backwardness in the path of my
revolution
I will continue

~~~~~
~~~~~

<u>A new reading of Abu Lahab's life story</u>

From our neighborhood mosque
Abu Lahab comes out
He wears Islam like a dress
And gold necklaces
He is a hypocrite, he backbites, he commits
adultery
He boasts that he has lineage
He locks his wife in a serf
He buries his daughter in the soil
Abu Lahab embodies Arab history
It is present everywhere
In mosques.....
In brothels
...and in cans
Available in government
And on the side of the road
And among the garbage... what a wonder
ladies and gentlemen
Abu Lahab declared his conversion to Islam
ladies and gentlemen

Islam is innocent of Abu Lahab
Abu Lahab rides the latest cars and eats the crusts
of civilization
Abu Lahab... marries four women
According to Sharia...
He says... Islam has been legislated
Abu Lahab defends the Messenger
And tears flow from his eyes
So you think he is Omar or Abu Bakr
Or God...how amazing!!!
Abu Lahab declares that he is with the revolution
After he fucked the people
Abu Lahab grows his beard and becomes a Salafist
All upon request!!
He raises slogans of freedom
Sometimes you see him demonstrating
Sometimes you see him bombing people
Sometimes you see him leading the worshippers
Sometimes you see him ringing the bell of anger
Abu Lahab sits like a corpse
...in cafes...

He gets drunk...and eats grapes
Abu Lahab is chattering......
And he backbites people
Abu Lahab eats his body with scabies
Abu Lahab loves like sheep, fucks like sheep,
and suffers from rabies
Imagine...
Abu Lahab now has a nickname
Abu Thaer....Abu Kasser
Abu killer.... Abu donkey
Wow.....Wow
Abu Lahab blindly imitates
Western civilization
Abu Lahab.. wearing a luxurious uniform
over his rotting pants
O Abu Lahab......
Please clean up your retarded mind
Before wearing a dress embroidered
with diamonds and gold
You ask me...
Who is Abu Lahab?

So I tell you
It's me.....it's you
It is the present of the Arabs

~~~~~

</div>
~~~~~

<u>Should we wait for WikiLeaks documents?</u>
<u>So we know we are stupid</u>

Should we be registered in the Guinness Book of
Records?
To know that we really hit the record for stupidity
Should we wait for Christ?
Or for the sky to collapse on us
Or we wait for the Mahdi to come to us
He was already disgusted and vomited when he
came
Syrians, Syrians.. My Syria!
We repeat it among the dustbins in the depths of the
epidemic
I am with the truth.. Badri told it
The stupid girl cried, hugging the flag
The soldier defected from the army
The other slapped his face as if he were in Karbala
Karbala you say!! O infidel, O Magi!
Children die and women are raped, "he says"
If you don't know, then you know

If you know, put a shoe in your mouth
Even if you know that you know
Is there any immorality after this immorality?
The nations of the earth are manipulating us
And they try their muscles on us
Not only the army is defecting
Rather, our asses defected from the severity of the
kicks
I will tell you the story of Khadija
She was with Tahseen in a stable life
Tahsin carried the hose on her
He hit her with a chair and hit her with a belt
Khadija revolted, Khadija screamed
Help me, O people of the earth and the heavens
Help came for Khadija
A war broke out and the children died
Thaer, the sweetheart, came to her
So smile at him, Hayat
Khadija felt sorry, Khadija regretted it
She longed for the days... she went into silence
Khadija was fed up.. Khadija shouted

Stop the farce, you scoundrels
They beat Khadija and humiliated Khadija
They dragged her by her hair from the Nile to the
Euphrates
Do you reject Thaer, Khadija?
He was your lifeline!!!!
He freed you, he pampered you
Is it him or someone who has displaced you on the
streets?
Would you say yes?
...Aren't you ashamed? Shut up
Don't you know him!! !! Ask Najat about him
Thaer loves you very much, Khadija
That's why he ruined your life
Thank him very much, Khadija
Marry him and Jihad
Do you refuse, Khadija
... Okay
I'll show you my other side

<u>Diary of an Eastern mongrel</u>

The narrator said, "Oh gentlemen, oh noble ones,
Enter Shahriar into the sheepfold,
And for a thousand years he has suffered
From tuberculosis, scabies, and backwardness,
Poverty in dignity, and leprosy.
And Scheherazade married him
With the law of idols.
For a thousand years,
Shahriar has loved like sheep, fucked like a sheep
imprisoning Scheherazade in the pen,
Treating her like sheep.
Oh gentlemen, oh noble ones,
Scheherazade gave birth to a mongrel resembling
his father,
What the fuck!
Grew up in a culture like vomiting and cold,
He went to school with a cold,
And he was raised like his father in the sheepfold.
He had a sister

Fed her for years in the pen
To face a death sentence
And the days went by...
And the sister loved an animal from another pen
And love is forbidden among women in the pen.
Anyway... that mongrel slept with her and left her,
And distributed her pictures
in the cheapest media.
Her brother, the cur, as usual,
Follows this media,
And pride grew in the cur
To slaughter her in the ugliest ways of crime.
The other mongrel "the judge"
reduced his sentence
under the pretext of an "honor killing."
Cursed be his honor, cursed be
That dark law, that Eastern law,
Surrounded by a thousand question marks,
An Eastern mongrel commits adultery and is
forgiven!

And a female is raped and faces a death sentence.
That Eastern cur commits adultery in the
application of Islam,
A time of Bedouin barbarism,
A time of humiliation and surrender.
The narrator said, "Oh gentlemen, oh noble ones,
Divided into a thousand pens...
Sorry, into a thousand religious sects
The religion of Islam,
Abu Lahab's created a sect,
Abu Jahl's created a sect also,
Even al-Mutanabbi and Abu Tammam!
A sect that kills, a sect that commits adultery,
And another sect that worships camels and
livestock!
Islam is innocent of all of you, motherfuckers.

<u>Diary of a Terrorist</u>

In your name, I kill
In your name, I fornicate
In your name,
I shed the blood of anyone who sings
They called me a terrorist!
Order me to kill
My trust in you will not be disappointed
Oh my lord, forgive me for killing children
Oh my lord, do not hold me accountable for my folly!
Oh Sheikh, grant me a seat in paradise
And take everything from me.
For you are the descendant of the prophets
You are the one guided from heaven
Let them say what they want about me
I will kill children and women
If I succeed, it's because of you
And if I err, it's because of me!
I will turn the land of Islam into Karbala

I will carry death with me to the islands
To Iraq, to Syria, to Sinai
If I enter paradise, it's because of you
And if I curse your father, it's because of me
The official speaker, you are in the name of
heaven?
A speaker on behalf of God, you sons of the bitch?
Your father is a sinner and your mother is a whore
You, who were rejected by everyone on earth and
in heaven
Are you killing to enter paradise, you sons of
ignorance?
Is this what you do wish?
Oh Sheikh, wearing desert clothes
And proclaiming himself a sultan
Glory be to the one who made the lowest among
the people our leader!
Oh Sheikh, found us among in garbage
And on hatred and hatred raised us
From the embrace of a whore comes

And takes the slogan "There is no god but Allah"
Is God speaking?
Or is it a directive from Sharon, our lord?
Oh my master, oh my dear sheikh
If you ever fought an invader to erase our sins
If you threw a stone to liberate Al-Aqsa
If you carried a child one day
To teach him the true religion and the Quran
you would be nobler than anyone on earth and
more pious
and on religion, we would be brothers
But you kill yourself
And in the end, we both die.

<u>The Poet and the Land</u>

He was a poet with a poem in his mouth
He used to sing
Wandering in a distant land
Dreaming of a hut in his homeland
With a bird whose song he hears in the morning
Dreaming of his father harvesting the land
And his mother smiling
And his little sister playing happily in the meadows
He returned like the wind searching for his home
For a buried toy and a neighbor's house
For his mother and his father in the harvest
For the bird singing and for his only sister
The soldiers burned down his home
And killed his sister
His father disappeared and his mother was lost
They destroyed the bird's nest
And the poor poet wandered like a madman in the
neighborhood
Nothing but his mother's scarf and his sister's toy

And his father's broken sickle
And blood on the vast land
The poet gathered his dreams
After the poem dried up in his mouth
He threw away his notebook and pens
With fire in his eyes and revenge on his mind
He screamed amidst the storms
For the poet was skilled in poetry
But death today is his skill
He embraced the earth as a martyr fell
His soul soared
May his wounds heal one day
And the house be rebuilt and the poem return
May the night of the homeless end
And a new dawn and new joys
The poet sang his last song
And the whole world echoed his anthem
Oh brother.. if your father, mother and sister died
What do you want other than revenge!

Abu Lahab attends Arab summit meetings

Singing foolishly to the rhythm of the mijwiz

Oh people of Arabness

In this summit, who are we?

Decisions and rejection

While Hulagu is in our bedrooms

We sing Arabness!

While unity dies beneath our horses' hooves

An Arab summit and speeches waste our time

Great nonsense, so what can words do to heal our
wounds?

Surrender and petty peace treaties

We reclaim our land with them

We beg the Jews and kiss their feet

To reclaim what is ours!

Oh Arab summit, what have you done to us!

We sold swords

And on the remnants of dates, we killed each
other!

We stepped on roses

and handed over to Abu Lahab
The banner of our Islam
Khalid kills Ali and Hamza kills Adi
So how can love be sung here?
Umar was killed, Uthman was killed, Ali was killed
Oh my God, what is happening to our history?
We returned to ignorance
And rebuilt our idols
Dahis, Al-Ghubra, and Bassous wandered among
us!
Do Hajjaj, Saddam, and Satan deserve
To be our leaders!?
Oh Arabs..
The stick deserves to be slapped on our backs
For without the stick, we would have made our
God from dung
Without the stick, we would have devoured each
other like dogs
The saying is true: We blame the times
But the times have no fault except with us.

<u>The poem wants to violate everyone's virginity</u>

Why do we die?
In one of the demonstrations
We shouted
We are donkeys
We never knew what we had done
We turned to the government
And we were accused of being mouthpieces of the
regime
We went to prayer
and they said we were ISIS
We turned to Ali
And we were killed by Muawiyah
We turned to Yazid
And we were slaughtered at the hands of Hussein
We resorted to demons
And by the hands of angels we were raped
We took refuge with the Taghlib tribe
And the Bakr tribe became angry with us
We took refuge with Quraysh

And from there we were expelled like dogs
We read the Qur'an
And they called us terrorists
We wrote a love poem
And they said we are heretics!
So excuse us if we disavow
From all of you
Forgive us if we spit
Forgive us if we hate you all
And we hated ourselves
If we are sadistic and illiterate
Bedouin and bloody
Don't blame us
You are the ones exploiting the mosques
And you, rulers of the East
You who use us
I am not one of you
So say about me, you are not one of us
You are all scum
Who gave you the right to represent us?
O you who kill and you who are being killed

If we fuck with your minds, forgive us
Forgive us if we curse your fathers and rest
A thousand dictators who shed our blood
Since we were born
Forgive us if we smash your empty heads and
rejoice
We gave our necks to devils and angels
We were not safe
Forgive us if we fuck
The mother of the government
And the mother of the demonstrators
And the mother of the conspirators
And the mother of the militants
And the mother of all
Forgive us if we burn you all
And we got burned
A thousand corpses rotting all the time
Forgive us if we violate
The virginity of the murderer and the virginity of
the murdered
Forgive us if we rape

We die like slippers
We thought ourselves martyrs!
Oh, you armed man!
Oh, security thugs
Both of you, relieve us of your immorality
O Easterner!
Bring yourself down while bringing down the
regime.
Drop the mind of adultery
We are insignificants
The ruler is no better than us
I wonder why you have killed this country
repeatedly
Why do these people flounder like drunkards?
Why do we die like shoes?
In the fucking East
Is the killer a criminal or the murdered?
The siege of soil has intensified
And killers roam around our graves
Like wolves
Mourners mourn their dead

And they fall like flies
No one cares about our death
Neither Ali nor Muawiyah
Not even Ibn Al-Khattab
No one writes a eulogy about us
Neither Jarir nor Al-Farazdaq
Nor Ziryab
No one heals us
Or he shoots us with a bullet of mercy
And relieves us from this torment
No one is afraid of a day of reckoning
Even a sheikh among us is a liar, the son of a liar
A thousand corpses on the road
They are thrown like animals
Then the dictator comes out
He gives us a speech
who are you ???
I say it as the liar once said it
Where are you going?
O minds that deserve to be raped
If you were not tyrants

In your homes
You surround your women and children with spears
If you were not Bedouins, you would wear the best
clothes you have over your rotten bodies
If you didn't destroy half of society
Your women
Through customary and temporary marriage, and
honor killing
And oppression behind doors
I would have been the first to shout with you
To establish a state for parties
You are all killers
Do not blame the bastard governor
If he steps on you
And he rips your flesh with his fangs
You will all fall into hell
You sons of dogs
You're all fuckers
murderers, scumbags
And your sheikh is a fraud
What can I say about our time?

In Iraq, killing based on identity
In Palestine, they trampled each other
And they forgot the issue
In the Udhra tribe
Qais rapes Laila
And she's still screaming
Oh Moatasem
There is no Mutassim
There was no savior until she fell captive
Who killed Duaa?
Or is her blood wasted?
Aren't you people with ignorant minds?
Who killed Elham?
Security, informants, conspirators, or thugs?
You are all killers
And your ruler is like you
You who claim civilization and peace
Elham Who stole her childhood?
And kill her... Answer me
You who go out in peaceful demonstrations
If there is justice

God will make the earth eclipse
Under the feet of the ruler and the people
A wicked time
Is the defect in time, as Al-Shafi'i said?
Or is the defect in our illiterate minds?
Where are our poets?
To say a word of truth
Or have their minds become despicable?
Jarir is still busy with satire
Al-Mutanabbi is still licking the shoes of Saif al-
Dawla al-Hamdaniya
As for Al-Hussein, he is still screaming
Everyone abandoned him
And they trampled on him
During a peaceful demonstration
O ruler
To reform your people drowned in blood
And terrible death
Kill your dogs
deploy the money fairly
And do not go hungry your people

Autumn will never end
Except by the law of spring
Heal their wounds
And teach them love
If you want, you can
Save from the cold the citizens
who are shivering in the cold
Extend your hand
No sane person will reject it
I am the first to obey
My last and most important message
to all
Is this freedom what you ask for?
Or is it herd instinct?
Don't take it from me
But the Prophet said
Beware of a terrifying time comming

~~~~~
~~~~~

<u>One day, people gathered as usual on Fridays with the venerable Sheikh</u>

He addresses them and teaches them
He guides them to religion and the principles of
interpretation
He sneezes and they applaud his sneeze
They are impressed by his height and long beard
The sheikh's face turned yellow one day while
reciting verses
The audience was really moved by that scene
And the wailing intensified
The sheikh said, with tears streaming down his
cheek:
Support your brothers in the Middle East, and
everyone rose up in revolt
To prepare their horses
He told them: Prepare aid, yourselves, and your
weapons
They liberated the country from the enemies of
God
In this holy month

One of the attendees said
Who do you mean by enemies of God?
Do you mean Israel!!
Everyone turned to him in amazement
As if from another planet
Or as if he was a genie who appeared at the end of
the night
The sheikh inadvertently farted from the horror of
the suddenness
Then he rose up screaming
Get this punk agent out of here

~~~~~
~~~~~

<u>After all the rants and chatter</u>

A cow emerged from the rubble
Making good a bad thing
He said about half the universe that they are
heretics
He made religion a store
He used religion as a means to justify the ends
He built a cemetery for freedom
He claimed to be from the Victorious Sect
Like a donkey, he snorted
He farted, showed off, and exploded
The people screamed when they heard his farts:
"Allahu Akbar"
Everyone came to support him
He laughed at the numbed crowd
People died in a massacre
He cried over them and became sad
He traded in their blood
Al-Mahdi came out, spat on them, and committed
suicide
The file became in the hands of charlatans and

magicians
what a beautiful, perfect ending!
the height of cynicism

~~~~~
~~~~~

<u>My country is addicted to war</u>
<u>Just as a prostitute is addicted to adultery</u>

And in this fucking country, I got dirty
I no longer know who I am
My heart is empty and my hands are cracked
And I am satisfied with this wealth
Syria is like a little girl
Bleeding on my hand, and screaming
She pray to God
Our fingerprints are everywhere
And her blood is on our shirts
Confession is inevitable
You and I killed her

~~~~~
~~~~~

<u>It is not a problem</u>
<u>Whether I come back or not</u>

Who cares ? Whether I die or not
We are like homeless dogs
We die on the side of the road
In my country, wc arc all children of monkeys
A country where the law of the jungle prevails
If the lion does not eat us, then for sure
The whale will swallow us...
Even if the sky does not fall on us
We'll fall into the groove
Even if the sons of Israel do not fuck us
The people of Sodom will fuck us
This is how our story began
Like the people of Aad and Thamud
And I'm lost alone
I am searching for a lost homeland
My heart is beating
My head is held high
My way is blocked

<u>I wanted to teach women human rights</u>

I wanted to teach them
That love is not practiced in a cage
Rather, in the plains, mountains and valleys
But they left me behind
And worshiped Satan
I wanted to teach the female
That the breast was not created for breastfeeding
But to fly
I tried to speak to their minds
To make them think with pride
I tried to get them out of the coop
And clean what is around them
From vomiting and worms
I got very tired ...
to convince her that she is a human being
One of them smiled stupidty and she said:
Yes Yes
She then carries the bucket
To clean the place

I'm tired of telling them
That what is in the tunnel are just rats
I tried to convince them
That their femininity
is a religion more important than all religions
I tried to convince them
To read Surah An-Nisa
Or Surah Ar-Rahman
But they married according to the Sunnah of God
and His Messenger
But after they distorted the Qur'an
I tried to ignite a revolution in them
Against the tribesmen
And to declare disobedience among them
I tried to convince one of them
To burn herself to begin the uprising
And for the tent to catch fire
She also laughed stupidly
To light a fire under the soup
Because her idiot husband is hungry
And another one, I'm tired of convincing her

That what she feels is not love
But delirium
She said stupidly
leave me alone
I am like him
I'm an idiot and he's an idiot like me
And my beloved loves me as I am
And I am very satisfied with my stupidity
I tried to convince onother woman
That her body is not food for men
But a flower
She also said stupidly
Yes Yes
And she fed her leaves and nectar to a coward
Some girl loved me
She loved the culture in me, or she claimed it
She really loved me? not important
The lesson is in the endings and the end is denial
She was uncultured
So I taught her breasts to write
Her breasts were ignorant in the past

I fed them grapes and raisins
I planted their land with coral
Then she raised the banners of freedom to please
me
She broke the bars of her prison and tore her shroud
She took part in demonstrations against polygamy
And honor crimes
She read to my satisfaction the teachings of
Confucius and Buddha
And world cultures
And she learned to play so she could play for me
Her most beautiful melodies
She demanded that poets rule the world
To decorate it with the most beautiful colors
But in the end
she left me after giving me a stroke, polio, and gout
She mocked my principles and my poetry
She threw down the flags of freedom
She mocked the teachings of Confucius and my
teachings
She stepped on Buddha's books

And she married her killer, the jailer
What a humiliation?
What a rottenness?
I tried to extract from women's bodies
Honey and basil
But they preferred to vomit
They chose to defecate
or let me shut up
Whatever...
I tried to convince them
To read a book
Instead of cooking zucchini and eggplant
I tried to take off their dusty clothes
To dress them in the dress of poems and crowns
I tried to make them wear a sun bracelet
the stars, planets, and cosmos
But they left me
And they sold their underwear
And their hearts and minds
In the sheep market
In this country of mine

A woman is equal to an animal
Any mule with a marriage certificate rides on her
She wears her wedding ring and handcuffs
She wears her impalement
with face smiling with contentment
In this country
The males of the family inherit the females
Such as furniture, tables and spoons
And the pictures on the walls
One takes his cousin
One takes his mother
Or his sister
Like a mule, like an animal
In this country
Males in it
A third of them cry and a third of them commit
adultery
The last third are like stray dogs
And girls in it
A third of them are weirdo and a third of them I
don't know how they think

The last third are locked behind walls
So I ask your permission, oh women of my tribe,
for me to leave
From your east
And all the countries in it
I ask your permission
To get rid of the dryness of your minds
And from my heavy burden of sorrows
I ask your permission
I don't have time to teach you
And experimenting with the experimenter
My nails have grown long while I am educating
you
The currency changed and my hair and beard grew
longer
My life is lost
It's time to change the adress
I ask your permission, my love
To take a long vacation from you
To oblivion
I ask your permission

To leave you, your kitchen, your bedroom, your
mind, and all universes.
I am tired of your thinking, which has become like
a horseshoe
I love you but I don't see you
Are you there
But I wonder!! Anywhere?
Let me drink my coffee
And leave
And read your cup as usual after I leave
I am afraid of the sea of your heart and mind
It's big, but...
it does not quench the thirsty
It is inhabited by scorpions, poisonous plants,
ghosts, and whales
I will escape from your sea
I don't want to become a pirate

~~~~~
~~~~~

<u>Rotten marriage</u>

In a house full of ignorance
Infested with rot and disease
People and everyone gather
They were like camels and cattle
And in a room of humiliation
A girl who lived delusions
Around her is an old hag
She hasn't showered in a year
And a matchmaker whose shape is like a bucket
You can't look at her because of its ugliness
They came to dye her face with henna
And to wash her breasts and feet
In the house, a cursed voice rose from a person
who looked like a mule
At the wedding sush as tragedy and drama
And a silly drum-like person carrying a drum
Like a goat playing tunes
One jumps like an animal
One howls
Another works as a servant

A farce under the name of wedding
And an idiot sheikh
He works in the afternoon as an imam
Whoever looks at him thinks he is Abu Bakr
Or Omar, or God
O Sheikh of customary marriage
And temporary marriage
Spread Islam in the world
You, the dirtiest slaver on earth
Leave God's religion alone
And worship stone
And an insignificant groom
Like a washed rat
He radiates majesty and honor
Oh rat, how beautiful and elegant you are
There is vomit and leprosy in your suit
The neighborhood's men gathered
A mule, a donkey, a cockroach, and a sheep
the Sheikh and the neighborhood men
They are nothing but dwarves
And a singer dancing like a drunkard, braying

God damned this wedding
It brings together all kinds of animals
What an oriental wedding like mold
It contains all diseases
It includes vomiting and tuberculosis
It has AIDS
It contains the disease of schizophrenia
You Easterner
who commits adultery in secret
and pretends to be pure in public: fuck you
O oriental female!
Take off the dress of tragedy
revolutionary against the wedding of rot
against the wedding of insects
revolutionary
against your killer, your seller, and your buyer
against all the scoundrels
And kill the pimp sheikh

~~~~~
~~~~~

<u>Scenes from our neighborhood</u>

The wind howls behind her and the braid
The breast is thrown to the dogs for a few pennies
And the man in our neighborhood has lost his
manhood
And his wife is at home, pregnant and humiliated
She prays to God to give her patience
He hears the morning news like a crocodile
Nothing in the world moves him
Even if a thousand people were killed
He sings with his echoing voice
He smokes tobacco and hookah
Suddenly a petty person comes
And screaming:
O Akid of our neighborhood, O Abu Dabbah
Come and see what your daughter did
He revolts like a thug
He sticks a long knife into her heart
Akid of our neighborhood, is a barking dog
He considers his victory over a woman a heroism!
You symbols of rottenness, O insignificant tribe

History will not rest from you
The house in our contry produces a thousand
insignificant people
The occupation's shoes will not move away from
you
it will always trample on you
You have no surah, no verse, no chapter
Neither the Qur'an nor the Bible
So arise, beautiful woman of my tribe
Marry Akid of tribe
prostrate to him, respect him, and wash his feet

~~~~~
~~~~~

<u>Love.. politics.. and adultery</u>

Since poems are dead
The time for talking is over
Since the love songs are exhausted
There was no time for her anymore
Since all the words of love were said
She burned and her time passed
Since my fingers are paralyzed
And my voice was assassinated
When I tried to write a bold love poem
Or a poem in which I express my weakness and
sadness
And my revolution against oppressors of my nation
I'm trying now
To search for a new way of loving
And to discover new words of love
I say it to my beloved in my own way
Words... that were never said in history except to
her
I'm trying to burn all the old love poems
And all the old love stories

And cowards are among its heroes
I'm trying to kill Antara...and Qais
And the petty womanizer
And all those who claim love
Those who make love like Bedouins and fools
Who devour four women
Who apply Sharia law with a Bedouin mentality
And they fucked up in applying it..
I try to burn all the love letters
Which were written throughout history
And all the meanings of immorality
Which hides between its lines
I'm trying to eliminate all the world's languages
And invent the alphabet of love
An alphabet without letters and without words
An alphabet that summarizes all languages
And the whole world understands it
I am trying to overthrow the old dictatorship of
love
I'm trying to kill it's ruler
I'm trying to kill the eaters of women flesh among

its inhabitants
I'm trying to turn history back
To relieve the Virgin of her sorrows
I'm trying to wander in the Arab desert
And among its tribes
I found the sheikh of the tribe burying his daughter
For fear of shame
So I feel mad and angry
And i turn the desert over heads of its people
And i burn Bakr and Taghlib
Qahtan and Quraish
And all its men
And bury all their nobles under its soil
I'm trying to enter the Caliph's palace
To complain to him
And to explain to him the nation's concerns and
sorrows
But the Caliph's guards expel me and kicks me out
of the palace
I insist on meeting the Caliph
They insist on expelling me

They give me two choices:
Either I go away
Or they will step on my neck
If it were up to me
I would have met the Sultan
And I will tell him:
Oh Sultan
There are a thousand criminals and a thousand
thugs around you
And thousand murderers and a thousand cowards
O Sultan
This people are hungry and oppressed
Your people have had their tongue cut out
If you want for this people to live in safety
Open the doors of your palace
And kill your thug guards
Be a compassionate
Be the human leader
Then be completely confident that we will win
And we say goodbye to all sorrows

~~~~~
~~~~~

<u>Crocodiles and the rose</u>

They killed the little girl, Elham
They drove her like animals
To the execution platform
They killed her
While holding in their hands the banner of Islam
They killed her in the presence of the official
And the presence of two witnesses
And the media
ladies and gentlemen
Don't look too much for evidence
And the witnesses
When the investigator took the fingerprints
He saw the effects of all of you
At the scene of the crime
He saw vomit
After analysis and auditing
He saw the fingerprints of the sheikhs of Islam
Where are you, our mother Aisha?
To see this rot and leprosy
They did not understand anything about your

biography
Except to get thier daughters married before
weaning them
Our sheikhs did not understand of religion
Except fatwas on how to enter the bathroom
Don't be surprised, mother
If we forget Gaza
We were busy breastfeeding the elder
And drinking the urine of camels
Oh our mother Aisha.. disown us
Tell your husband
Tell the best of God's creatures, Prophet
Muhammad
Tell him not to intercede for us
And not to look at our faces
We are all sons of haram
Tell him that we are the most impure nation in the
world
Over the days
Tell him that his efforts to spread religion were in
vain

We still worship stones
Tell him to close the gates of heaven
The Day of Resurrection is in our faces
And in the faces of the sheikhs of darkness
Tell Abu Hanifa, Al-Shafi'i and Ali:
After you, there are no sheikhs left
But just a fools and contemptible persons
O mother, spit in our faces
After God has acquitted you
We still accuse you of adultery
We are still exploiting the story of your pure
marriage
To justify our sinful actions
After God forbade slavery
We still enslave our women
Oh our mother
Step on the chins of our sheikhs
In this era, we are urinating from our heads
In this era, we now defecate from our mouths
O pure one!
Oh our mother

Tell the messenger
To turn back time
To be sent to others
To be sent among the Mongols or the Jews
Or even in Gog and Magog
But not between us
Tell him to pray to God
To eclipse the earth beneath us
Oh our mother Aisha
Don't pay attention to us
We are crocodiles
We are all like dung of cows
Even demons disavowed our actions
What is the fault of that little girl?
To die under our feet
Oh Aisha, oh our mother
You married the Messenger by inspiration from
God
God has married you to the Prophet
so that you can preserve the religion and convey it
to us

But we forgot religion
We turned religion into adultery
True... Elham was killed
At the hands of criminals
But the issue is bigger than an incident that
happens there or here
The issue is the daily terror we practice on our
women
The issue is thousands of roses dying
under the feet of animals in our east
The issue in Sharia law is that we have turned it
into a bar
where we can have sex with each other
The issue is divine wrath
In God's vengeance
Which will soon descend upon us
Oh Elham
A drop of blood dripped from your vagina
Before your death and after your death
More honorable than all the prayers of our sheikhs
A hair on your head

More honorable than all our nobles
Oh Elham
In Paradise, tell your mother Aisha and our mother
That darkness fell between us after you
One or more Elham exist
In every one of our homes
We took the religion from the Messenger
And when we applied it
Our eyes became blind
And we have became donkeys
Rather, donkeys are better than us
And we died and our skins rotted
Oh Elham, pray to God
That our bodies will never be buried

~~~~~
~~~~~

<u>When the rose is violated (1)</u>

I dreamed of a legendary knight
one of the noblest human beings
holds my hands and hugs me
wipes a tear from my cheek
And his words are like raindrops
I dreamed of a real man
carries me to a high heaven
to narcissistic forests
makes me hear the chants of roses
teaches me the names of birds
And all the languages of trees
I dreamed of a love that lights up my dark skies
Forgives me every sin
It relieves me of hours of sadness and boredom
I dreamed a lot
And now I am a captive slave
At the filthiest human being
Prison bars around me
And the executioner is my husband
He looks at me

In the other room there are three women
He sits like a corpse
He violates me
And he throws his body at me
With all his psychological and sexual complexes
With all that he inherited from the barbarism of the
Tatars
Four women were given to him by Sharia law as a
gift
A breast here and a lip there
This is how Sharia is exploited by a dirty Easterner
Didn't that bastard know?
Islam is a gift from heaven
Not to satisfy his sadistic desires
Not to his Bedouin mentality
And his rotten heart
Glory be to Him who made this animal rule over
me
and made his mistakes and vices forgiven and
forgotten
And made my mistakes unforgivable!

He is a Muslim by identity
His four wives are legal
He takes each of them for sexual exploitation
It bears the ugliest behaviors of the Mongols
Thc filthiest pre-Islamic morals
And the most impure actions of the gypsies
People, don't be unfair to me
I am not a Whore
This Easterner believes in four women
But he does not believe in God

~~~~~
~~~~~

<u>When the rose is violated (2)</u>

We are women of the East
We have no homeland
We are sold in the slave market in the name of
marriage
And the father received the price
We are trapped and oppressed
Love in our country exists in a shroud
We are like slave girls
Father signs our marriage certificate
He sends us on a moonless night
To our destruction
To a man without a heart, without a mind
We are women of the East
We have no homeland
We have given our bodies to the Beloved
He left after sleeping in our bed
So we repented and God forgave our mistakes
But the headsman was waiting for us
Where is comfort and where is safety?
So why did our men become like animals?

They commit adultery but do not forgive our mistakes
Does the real man in our time not exist?

~~~~~
~~~~~

<u>When the rose is violated (3)</u>

We are the women of the East
East of backwardness and hatred
We are treated like the offspring of a slave girl
We are sold like commodities in slave markets
Zaid and Abu Al-Atahiya rape us
We are handed over to the rabble of the desert
If we wear the hijab, they say
She's retarded and ISIS
If we reject the restrictions, they say:
She's stupid
And if we were naked, they would say
She's a whore
O men of my tribe
We disown you
Consider it impoliteness
They considered it selfish
Say whore, say slut
Say: an adulterer
I am free, not a slave
God is my Lord

My idol is the Virgin Mary
I am free like a fish in the sea
Like mountain flowers
Say whatever you want about me
I don't care
It is enough for me
that I am the granddaughter of the Virgin Mary
And Fatima Al-Zahra

~~~~~
~~~~~

<u>They stole my childhood</u>

My past is linked to the Arabs
But the tragedy of the Arabs is the present
My mother was honored in the West
Here they accused her of impoliteness
I toured the East
From India
To the land of Al-Hatta and Al-Aqal
From the country of Sindh
To the Sublime Porte
From the Kurdish land
To the land of outdated thought
From the land of oil to the land of gold
I did not find any brains
But piles of garbage
I found calves and mentally disturbed men
I found an ogre beating his wife
and fucks her like mules
i found the east not changed
it still suffering for a thousand years
From scabies...

I returned home
I brushed the dust of fatigue off my forehead
I looked for my neighbor
That good man
I searched in the cold for a wood stove
They told me that he died of cold and hunger
A long time ago..
Half of its people were displaced
Half of them emigrated
Abu Lahab bought his house
I asked about Gulnar
They said that she married Abu Lahab
I was surprised.. they said
Is there anyone in the neighborhood who does not
know Abu Lahab!?
He is that fraudster who made a fortune through
bribery
Looting and plundering
I asked about Hind, Laila, and Farah
They answered me that all of them married Abu
Lahab

I asked about the childhood garden
They said: Abu Lahab burned it
In its place, he built a prison for his women
Next to it is a brothel
It is frequented by the most vulgar Arabs
I asked them about that worthless person standing
at his door
They said lower your voice
He works for Abu Lahab
He is the pimp of passion
And the owner of the beautiful handwriting
And the owner of the voice
He sings the worst types of singing
I asked them about a grave in which I should sleep
After years of fatigue
They laughed at me and said
There are no graves left
The graves of the whole country
belong to Abu Lahab
I looked at them
And tears have flowed from my eyes

I sat on a stone with angry signs on my face
They smiled and said:
It is not allowed to sit here
A decision issued by Abu Lahab
It is also not allowes to laugh or cry
Or get angry or die
Except with permission from Abu Lahab
I caught a jasmine and planted it in the ground
Next to a grape arbor
And I asked them... For heaven's sake, tell me
Who is Abu Lahab!?
So they took out their silencer pistols
And shut me up
And their knives cut my tongue
And they gouged out my eyes
They trampled on the jasmine that I planted
in its place they planted me..
And they accused me of heresy and treason
They screamed loudly
We are all Abu Lahab..
They killed my childhood

And they killed me
But I will rise from the dead
To take revenge on those who crucified me
I will rise like Christ
But not to forgive
But to gouge out the eyes of those who plucked out
mine eyes
to burn the earth under those who denied me not
only three times,
but a thousand
I will rise .. in the name of Julnar
Hind, Farah, and Asmaa
I will rise in the name of every flower that was
unjustly stoned
On a dark night
In the name of every flower that cries
And the sorrows of the Virgin Mary
In the name of the Arab Prophet
In the name of Christ in heaven
O Easterner!
Your enemy is not Israel

But is the worm
Which gnaws at your mind all the time
Your enemy is not that ant, elephant
As long as you are drowning in this nonsense
Clean your mind
Before Israfil bloew the trumpet
before the universe is engulfed in disaster
O Easterner!
You will not fight Israel
The Jews do not fight stupid peoples
Should I laugh at your long dark night?
Neither laughter nor crying will do you any good
Where are you, Gabriel?
To drown the entire East
God created the heavens and the earth
And he made Michael give sustenance
He sent messengers to end this dark night
Muhammad, Jesus, Moses, and Isaac
O East!
It is impossible to free your land
As long as you are immersed in backwardness and

hypocrisy
What is the benefit of reading the Qur'an and the
Bible?
As the Prophet said
If you don't understand anything from it
O Easterner! you useless one
O Bedouin!
Who dances on the ruins of his tent
And the ruins of his virginity
And the ruins of his disappointment
You retarded person
O you who lick the shoes of civilization
Wouldn't you know?
You are frivolous and backward
Wouldn't you know?
That you have tuberculosis, syphilis and leprosy
And your mind is bleeding
Wouldn't you know.. Wouldn't you know?
Time stopped centuries ago for you
Centuries ago
Your ass is on the impalements crawling

Your virginity has fallen and your breasts have
swelled
And your pussy is bleeding
You don't know yet!!
Then kill yourself
Just as you killed your sister before
End this shame

~~~~~

the end
~~~~~

Don't miss out!
Visit the website below and you can sign up to receive emails whenever khalil altahhan publishes a new obligation.

BOOKS 2 READ

https://books2read.com/r/B-A-EYQBB-PAZXC

Connecting independent readers to independent writers.

About the Author

Khalil Altahhan is a Syrian author. He was born in Damascus in 1984 and studied law at Damascus University before he was forced to emigrate due to the war. He writes novels and poetry, and expresses his feelings, experiences, and hopes through his words. He has two published novels, "The Prophecy of the Eternal Winter" and "Tears of Angels," and two books of poetry, "Before You Shed My Blood" and "Diary of a Damascene Wound." He is also working on finishing several other novels. His writing is inspired by the harsh conditions of life, war, asylum, and grief. He is a writer who graduated from the school of sadness and harsh life, and seeks to spread peace, love, and hope through his works. You can contact him via email: khalil4love@hotmail.com
Or follow his page on YouTube: youtube.com/@lover4damascus